Indian Gaming from an Indian:

Introduction to Indian Gaming

Published by

Native Thoughts Publishing

4772 Haxton Way

Ferndale, WA 98248

Text Copyright © 2016 by Aaron Thomas

All rights reserved. No part of this book may be reproduced or utilized in any form or by any means, electronic or mechanical, including photocopying, recording or by any informational storage and retrieval system without permission in writing from the publisher except for the inclusion of brief quotations in a review.

Printed in the United States of America.

Book Concept by Aaron Thomas.

This book is dedicated to those who have the passion to increase opportunities for tribes in the area of business, specifically gaming and hospitality.

"Indian Gaming from an Indian"

and to all tribal People

for you have so much resilience

and deserve the Earth and all that

it has to offer.

Prologue

When Indian Gaming came back onto the scene (at least for us at Lummi Nation in 1992), I was in high school. I remember our tribal leaders saying that gaming was going to take the place of the fishing industry by providing jobs and heck even a career path if we played our cards right. Lummi Nation was one of the only tribes in the United States that had over 600 purse seiner boats back in the 1980's, so saying that gaming was going to replace fishing for our tribal members was saying a lot...

Our first 'official' gaming effort, Lummi Casino, opened up in 1992 with over 20 table games. Slot machines were still not available to tribes and so we decided to take what the US Government 'would allow.' Table games did well for us, I mean, it was no slot machine, but in the end the profitability of it (albeit a bit volatile) would seem to grow for us.

Hundreds of thousands of new dollars was coming into the Lummi Nation and of course most of us didn't have a clue what to do with that new money. The biggest problem that we faced wasn't so much that the dollars that were coming in was a headache but our biggest problem...was quite frankly...US!

None of our tribal members (which at the time numbered a respectable 3,500 people and counting) had any real gaming operations experience. Heck, you look around today, some 20 years later and we still don't have a lot of our tribal members that have ever led or directed, much less managed a casino department.

In 1998, the same year I graduated with my Bachelor of Arts degree in Communications at Washington State University, we closed down the Lummi Casino. Although Vancouver, BC (which is about 60 minutes north of us) expanded gaming to allow Vegas-like slot machines, this was not the only problem. I am not underestimating the effect that their expansion had on us, but I believed and still believe that wasn't our main problem.

WE were the main problem; mainly because WE couldn't get out of the way of our own success.

I boil this problem down to one thing; our poverty mentality which limits us from envisioning that the dollars that we're getting could in fact double, triple or even break the ceiling on our bank vaults.

Poverty mentality says don't trust anyone. It screams out 'watch your back,' 'horde the information,' 'step on throats to retain your high paid positions,' and my favorite, 'no one working in a casino should make more than $50,000 per year and definitely not be paid bonuses!'

The flip side to the poverty mentality is an abundance mentality, defined as 'a mentality that envisions there is more than enough to go around,' 'a community of WE and not I,' 'mentorship versus dictatorship,' and my personal favorite 'if you make us money, in turn you will get more money.'

Our poverty mentality keeps us stuck down in the weeds and creates a 'crabs in the bucket' syndrome that won't allow our most prized and smart tribal members to get out of the bucket without someone trying to grab at their feet and bring them 'back to reality.'

I am very thankful that I come from a big family, eh' hem, a big LOVING family who have been my rock and my cheerleaders since I could remember. Education is a big theme in the Thomas family and I was the second in this big family to earn my Masters of Business Administration degree.

Having an MBA doesn't mean much, other than I've developed the tools to read, write and do some math. Having an MBA, however, also means responsibility, integrity and a duty to do whatever I can to help my tribe or whomever I am honored to work with.

I was able to get out of the bucket and spread my 'hawks wings enough to fly in and out of the business activities of four casinos. I am very thankful to the mentors who took me under their own wings and showed me things that I will never forget.

I've been in the gaming industry for over 12 years and even though I have earned my degrees, held some prominent casino job titles, made hundreds of thousands of dollars, I still don't know everything.

One of my mentors, Andy LaChapelle, once told me before he retired that he had been in the industry for over 30 years and he still found new casino information that baffled him. He was always quick to share his new insights with me, who at the time I was a budding executive who looked up to him like another father.

Andy would always tell me that I could read books, look at numbers until the cows came home, but the real learning was out there on the casino floor. You would always find Andy out on the casino floor going in and out of the slot machines, going behind the guests as they laid down another

$100 bill on the blackjack table, peering into the restaurants and talking to team members and guests alike.

Andy's big thing was headcounts, keeping track of how long it took to service our guests. Andy got it. He not only understood the dynamics of ensuring the wallets were emptied out of the guest's pocket and onto our craps table, but wanted to understand why headcounts were up on a particular Wednesday.

"Dude (for some reason, Andy always called us men 'dude'), what the heck did we do in Marketing yesterday?" Andy would sit across from your desk and if he really wanted to make a point, he would grab his chair and sit almost next to you to talk 'with' you, not 'down' at you.

Andy's only management weakness that I could see in the six years that I had a pleasure of working alongside of him was his temper. Andy's office was on the other side of a wall that divided our two offices and at least once a week, I could hear him yelling on the top of his lungs at one of his direct reporting team members about something he did wrong (it was always a 'dude' he would yell at and rarely, if ever, a woman).

I finally had to say something to our boss, the General Manager, about it. I told him that I didn't appreciate hearing yelling next door. What Harlan didn't know is that I grew up in a house that had domestic violence in it and I wanted to go to work to forget that part of my past and not be reminded of it.

Waking up at 3 AM with your dad yelling at your mom wasn't something that I was proud of (nor am I proud today about that) but unfortunately, for some, that's reservation life.

Reservation life meets business life was one of the hardest transitions of my entire life (so far? Lol.). Reservation life or rez life, as I call it, includes that poverty mentality that I was talking about earlier but it includes so much more, like domestic violence, drug addiction, suicide…and on and on.

Our tribal communities may have the lowest employment rates, highest suicide rates, and highest domestic violence rates per capita, but we also have the biggest hearts and the laughter from one rez family could shake a house.

I decided to write this book during the first year of my transition off the Lummi Rez. I had just left a high-responsibility job at our casino, where I was the Director of Marketing for almost 8 years.

I was forced out onto the sidelines, mainly because of my belief that we had non-gaming people trying to run our casino through a new General Manager who did in fact have gaming experience. I could see that the decisions the non-gaming people were making were going to cause the business to decline. We were becoming old Lummi Casino all over again, and for my own health and financial well-being, I decided to leave.

Writing this book has been therapeutic for me and I feel a general sense of pride at having been able to share my professional experiences with those who want to know more about this industry. It is my hope that this book will at least open the eyes up to tribal leaders, gaming executives and any persons currently working at or who want to work in a gaming facility.

As I attend state and national gaming conferences, there's not too many tribal executives (at least at the time of writing this book) that have any real gaming operations experience. I am truly one of the lucky and skilled tribal executives who knows first-hand what it's like to have to go through tough economic times as well as the happy times when the champagne was uncorked every January because we just broke another annual profit (EBITDA) record.

I hope that tribal members who read this book will get a better sense of what it truly takes to help a casino run more smoothly, to help grow their revenue and to lead with a business hat on rather than the political hat that we've become so used to in the tribal government sectors.

I wish you all well with your endeavors as you look to increase profit for your tribe. I hope that this book will serve as a book of guidelines that will propel you to the next level of your gaming knowledge.

In the Lummi language, we say 'hyshqe' which means 'thank you.'

Hyshqe siam e ne schaleche siam.

Thank you my dear friends and relatives. Thank you for buying this book and good luck on your gaming and business journey.

Aaron M. Thomas, MBA

Haw-het-ton

Table of Contents

Chapter I: What is Business?

Chapter II: Gaming and the US/Tribes

Chapter III: The Basics of Gaming

Chapter IV: Changing of Business Culture

Chapter V: Total Quality Management

Chapter VI: What is Profit?

Chapter VII: Marketing: Promotions, Reinvestment %, New players, New Whales

Chapter VIII: Yes, Data is for More Than Tribal Elections

Chapter IX: Guests' Interest and Profit

Chapter X: Per Capita

Chapter XI: How to Manage Stress in a Business Setting

Chapter XII: Don't be THAT Casino...!

Chapter I: What is Business?

I start with this topic because it is one that I feel most tribes have a challenge really understanding. Casinos are businesses, <u>not</u> another government service. Business-the true meaning of the word, not the type that most tribal governments claim they do, means something different. Moving papers around, acting like you are in 'business meetings' is not the definition of business…sorry if that offends.

Business creates value that other people want or need at a price they are willing to pay that satisfies their wants and needs so that profit is available.

Hmm..Business creates value that other people want. What do people really want? There are five core human drives:

1. Drive to acquire: physical and power needs
2. Drive to bond: a desire to feel valued
3. Drive to learn: desire to satisfy curiosity
4. Drive to defend: desire to protect ourselves.
5. Drive to feel: desire to new sensory stimulus, intense emotional experiences, pleasure, excitement, entertainment.

The more 'drives' you offer, the more attractive it will be to your potential market.

Out of all five of these 'drives', what do you think most affect gaming?

I would argue for #1 (the drive to acquire), #2 (the drive to bond or feel valued) and #5 (the drive to feel pleasure, excitement).

Our gaming industry dangles in front of the casino players the power to acquire things such as cars, trips, money. It also uses mailers and great face-to-face guest service to drive loyalty to our brand. Casinos use intense sensory stimulus to create emotional experiences through the billion lightbulbs in a slot machine and exciting build-up to a winner of big money during a casino promotion.

This, my fine feathered friends, is true business and when you get the bug to create new businesses, boy you better watch out.

There's nothing so powerful as having an idea, one that you know will cater to at least one of the five core drives of the human being and one that will make you a ton of profit.

Casinos also have the ability to help the guest feel valued. We teach our team members to use the guest's first name (since we have access to their ID which has their full name on it) and to smile and greet, to ask them if they need anything else and thank them or say good luck.

The drive to feel is evident from the excitement of the bells and whistles of our slot machines, the anticipation of the announcement of a new jackpot winner over the loud speaker and watching someone smile when they win a brand new car.

Again, these three core human drives help generate business and create value for our guests.

Now that we've gone over what business is, let's chat about what you should be looking for out of your casino in terms of financial statements that you can review monthly or quarterly:

Income Statement

One of the most important documents is the Income Statement. This is also known as the profit and loss statement (P & L Statement) or Operating Statement or Earnings Statement. This report is vitally important to know and understand because it will tell you what your net profit is from the business and after various accounting deductions, what amount of money your tribe's bank should expect to receive.

Your casino executives, who call the shots, should all have access to this information because it will give them a monthly (as well as daily and annual) at-a-glance summary as to how their teams did and thus where they may have succeeded and just as importantly, where they could improve.

You may have a CEO who tries to tell you that your revenue is up from a year ago (Year over year or Y-o-Y) and that you should be just fine with that. WRONG! Never, ever, ever, ever let your CEO tell you that revenues are up and let that be the end of the story.

An income statement will show you the revenue number that your CEO is raving about but it will also minus out the cost it took to get that increased revenue. These costs include: how much money to get the goods (Cost of Goods Sold), other expenses and taxes.

This is calculated in a common formula:

Revenue-Cost of Goods Sold-Expenses-Taxes=Net Profit.

Cost of Goods Sold is basically how much money it took to purchase the items that you sold for more money than you bought it for. For example, if a lamp cost you $10, (which is your Cost of Goods Sold) and you sold it for $15, then the cost of goods sold is $10, and the profit was $5.

Expenses include things such as payroll and other operating expenses; things that made your casino run in the first place, including: power/electricity to run your slots, the car your Marketing team gave away and so forth.

I think we all know about taxes, but since most tribal casinos don't pay taxes, we can probably erase that one out of the equation. Just know that taxes in non-reservation businesses are taken into account in the traditional P & L.

There are other items that you could look at but I don't want to inundate you with that right now. Soon, in another book, we'll delve into casino math and casino financing so that you can see other great tools to use to evaluate your business. Now, let's look at how we might use all of these numbers we get in the financial reports.

Trending Analysis

Ok, so now you've got your Profit and Loss statement. Now you can begin to chart how your business has progressed in the past: one, five and 10+ years (if your casino has been opened that long). You should be able to see what your casino did last year at that same time.

When you are reviewing the history of your P & L, look for any weird number that sticks out. Is one number way under or way over?

This is where your keen eye needs to look for this information and for your slick tongue to ask good questions (or any questions) of your CEO. He/She should have seen why a certain number is so different than the other ones and be able to answer to it.

Trending analysis is great for asking the question 'Why?' It's the 'why's' of the business that gets us to learn the most about ways we can improve or sustain the same type of items that got you there.

Businesses run on what is known as KPIs or Key Performance Indicators. Such indicators that most casinos look at are: payroll costs (usually the biggest number in your 'cost' section), slot revenue (including hold percentage or how much money the casino won in slots, WPU or Win Per Unit which is how much money each slot machine won in that gaming day), table games revenue, food and beverage revenue, marketing expenses (mostly controlled costs like advertising and promotions). KPIs are what every CEO looks at and every CEO has different ones that they review every day. KPIs are the 'KEY' performance indicators or what would happen if that key indicator went up or down to help drive revenue or reduce costs.

We'll get back to the numbers in the 'Data' chapter later on in this book.

Summary:

Key Points:

- Just know that business, true business, is way different than tribal government. Most decisions in business are done looking at numbers and more specifically the trend analysis as explained above.
- The P/L is a great tool to use to evaluate your casino's business over time.
- It's the 'why's' of a business that gets us all the details we need to strategize our next moves.

Questions to ask your CEO or other members of your upper management:

1. What is your year-over-year profit and loss tell you about our business?
2. Just because revenues are up, how much did it cost to get that much revenue?
3. Did our expenses rise and if so, where and why?
4. What do our trends say about our business?
5. What are our Key Performance Indicators that you look at and why?

Chapter II: Gaming and the US/Tribes

I remember when I was in my first week at one of the four casinos I worked with when my then Assistant General Manager, asked me if I had ever read the 'documents that hold us accountable to the US government.'

I remember getting a bit perturbed by that comment. I was fresh out of working at a different tribal entity which was deeper into the reservation than this casino and I to this day don't know why I would be upset about such a simple question?

What does any of that have to do with our role of getting more revenue for the tribe through gaming? I recalled asking that of the Assistant GM, who later would be a mentor and good friend.

He went on to explain that we cannot go further into our work at this casino without knowing and having a basic understanding of things such as Inherent Rights, Sovereignty, Self-Governance, Gaming Compacts and the all-important Treaties that were signed.

Inherent Rights

Let's start with the foundation of why we get to have gaming in the first place. I always hate saying 'why we get to have..' well, anything because as tribal nations, we should just be able to do what we want; but then you get into the whole 'well the US government was threatening to kill all of our people' discussion, and that pretty much ends that conversation.

According to Dictionary.com, the word 'inherent' means "Something that is permanent or an inseparable element."

So, one would argue that tribes' inherent rights are the rights they have that are permanent or never separate from them as a People.

Tribes have always contended that we had certain rights that we hold to be our truth since 'time immemorial' or since the beginning of our time on this earth.

Sovereignty

We hold these inherent rights close to our hearts because these rights always allowed us to do whatever we felt we needed to do to survive: fishing, hunting, praying, language, singing, dancing, etc. These inherent rights will never go away for as long as we live.

The ability to act on these inherent rights is our definition of sovereignty, which really means 'supreme power.' We have the supreme power to do what we need to do on our lands including the right to gaming.

Treaties

During the United States' campaign to go from what is now the East Coast and make their way West for their 'Manifest Destiny,' they had to come up with a way to keep peace between the tribes and the non-Indian people.

There had been numerous wars between the US and the tribes as the tribal nations did whatever they could to protect their lands, their women and children and their inherent rights.

To this day, I despise it when tribes 'celebrate' Treaty Day because those treaties were not in the best interest of our People. They were filled with 'deliverables' that the US Government either hasn't lived up to nor were those deliverables ever intended to be fulfilled.

To keep peace with most of you, however, I will go along with the spirit of it and say that Treaties were at a minimum designed to keep more of our people from dying. I'm thankful for that and still have a glimmer of hope that the US Government will honor each of them to the fullest intent of their meaning.

Self-Governance

Lummi Nation, where I'm from, was one of the tribes that adopted the idea that tribes could in fact take the Bureau of Indian Affairs (BIA) out of the equation. The BIA was created by the Federal Government to 'be the keepers of Indian Affairs' which was basically meant to do the President's dirty work and ensure that we as tribes stayed low key and didn't kill off any non-tribal people.

Self-Governance, had been a dream of the Lummi elders for quite some time. Before 'the right to govern ourselves' was recognized, my tribal leaders and those of other tribes' had to drive down to Everett, Washington or Portland, Oregon to get approval to spend money, to ask for money to get permits, and any other items to make the ends meet.

One day, in the 1980's, the tribes said it was our inherent and sovereign right to be able to conduct our own business to the best of our ability. We would be the keepers of our own way and conduct business, such as elections, managing our own tribal funds, healthcare, education, economic development, and so on.

It was here that I think we got it right, but it was also here in this point of time that the current erosion of our economic development process began. Why do I say that? When the crap was hitting the fan before self-governance, we could all unite against the dreaded 'big brother' called the US Government.

When you're under self-governance, you get to blame only one person…'yourself.'

It was also during this time that the US Government got smart and said, okay, if you think you can run your own damn tribe, then we'll make you all fight again for the limited amount of money that we already said we'd owe you under the treaty obligations.

This fight for limited funds opened up a can of worms that taught us how to step on each other's throat to get what we needed, to think in a poverty minded way (as I mentioned in my introduction), and for most tribes, to depend on the US government process: it's elections, and the humiliation of its 'stand in line with our hand out and hope to God that the US Congress votes in our favor to fund x, y or z'.

Indian Gaming Regulatory Act (IGRA)

Tribes were longing for a way to be able to fund themselves, and so just after some had decided to create a self-governing Nation, they also decided that they wanted to get into the gaming industry.

Gaming, considered by my tribe at least, was one of our inherent rights. We have a long and accustomed traditional game called 'Sla-hal,' or bone game, which was a guessing game using phallic looking sticks and hand drums.

Some tribes didn't want to wait for the 'good faith negotiations' that other tribes were engaged in with the US Government and decided to start a casino on their own.

They turned their local gymnasiums from a place where kids shot basketballs and instead bought craps and blackjack tables. For a short while, they were turning basketball hoops into hundred dollar bills, and just like that the first non-Vegas, non-Atlantic City casinos popped up in a few places around Indian Country.

At that time, President Ronald Reagan and his cabinet were not having that and so within a few months of getting wind that these tribes (including my own) were setting up shop, they sent the SWAT teams over to pay us a little visit.

They shut our first attempt at a full table games casino down, and just like that we were back to square one.

Again, since the tribes were very dependent on the US government for pretty much most things that needed funding, especially healthcare, they lobbied Congress to help them spur economic development through gaming.

In my humble opinion, the US Government was thinking, 'well heck, these tribes live so far into their territories and we placed them in high terrain or low lands that no one will ever want to go and visit them anyway…let's give them their damn sovereign right to gaming.'

So, in the mid-1980's the Indian Gaming Regulatory Act (IGRA) was born. It was also sold as a way to allow tribes to have gaming but actually it was a controlling regulation of a right we already used. The one caveat to having our own casinos was that since the Federal government didn't completely trust us, they ensured that we had to have good faith negotiations with each State government.

Some would argue that this piece of language was implemented as a means to have unity amongst the people who live in or near a newly formed casino, but we all know it was designed as a way to keep some of the profit involved at the State level; the State wanted their piece of the pie.

Gaming Compacts

What's scary about some tribal casinos is that I'm sure that most of the current General Manager/CEOs that are leading your casino (including the tribal members who are leading your casino or who are the business arm of the tribe) have no idea about what any of the history or terms that I've listed above.

One major component of how things work in gaming today are the Gaming Compacts that each of the tribes and the States entered into.

Again, the US Government wanted a good faith relationship between the tribes and the States, and so the US Government instituted the requirement to have gaming compacts written, negotiated and agreed to which would spell out how each party would conduct gaming on tribal lands.

These compacts are somewhat outdated, and at the time of writing this book, most tribes are in the process of re-creating their draft compacts for the States to review. It's important to get a hold of and review all of the documents that I've listed above, and this one in particular.

Gaming compacts, not only spell out each party's role, but it also talks about what each casino may offer. Things such as video lottery terminals (or slot machines), table games (what type depends on which tribe/state that they are in), and even more important, what types of games are not listed. It's important to review your legal documents, especially your gaming compact.

It's also key to know what your tribe may want to offer in the future. What if you wanted to offer sports betting or fantasy sports at your casino? You better begin with the gaming compact that your tribal council signed years back, and if you want it, have the balls to go after it and place it in your gaming compact.

Summary

It's imperative that all tribal casino owners know and have a basic understanding of these documents. They are the foundation as to how tribes may offer gaming and again, like my mentor told me, how are we supposed to know where we are going if we don't know where we have been?

Some important questions to ask your CEO or other leaders that are running your casino's day-to-day operations:

1. Name three key pieces to the IGRA and how do they apply to our casino?
2. In reviewing our Gaming Compact, what are some recommendations that you have to enhance our casino in the future?
3. What are inherent rights and how do they apply today to our businesses, specifically the casino?
4. What is the history of gaming in our tribe and how can we learn from our past to help us in the future?
5. How does the US elections process affect what we do here at our casino?

Chapter III: The Basics of Gaming

To understand gaming, you really have to be around it as much as you can. You can read this or other books, watch movies like *Casino*, but until you are there watching it, it may be difficult to understand how people react:

1. When they first enter your property.
2. When they get into one of your lines like the rewards club.
3. When they pay for their meal at the point of sale (POS) station.
4. When they lose at slots or table games.
5. When they win a promotional item on the casino floor.
6. When your entire casino floor goes down and doesn't allow your patrons to print out their slot ticket from the slot device.

....uh yeah, that last one is a real doozy.

Look, Listen and Learn

One of my mentors told me that paying close attention to this was one of the key elements to managing an effective casino floor and I believe it. I've been looking, listening and learning for years and what this really means is to not make any judgements on anything until you look at it, listen for feedback from your guests or your team members, and learn from what you are seeing and hearing.

Learning your casino floor is one of the key elements to understanding the basics of gaming. You can look and listen all you want but until you really write what you are learning down on paper, go back and follow up on it through an email, text, in-person (which I recommend the most) or a phone call, you won't really learn what is happening.

Being on your casino floor and really watching what is going on is key.

If you are a Council Member or on the business arm of your tribe, then you are a visible person in your community and people know who you are, you may want to be a little stealthy as to how you are doing this. You don't want to stand in the middle of your casino floor when you know that people see you and know that you are a key member in your community.

Why?

Understanding gaming starts with your team members. They are the ones who have been on your casino floor hundreds if not thousands of times before you decided to learn more about your product.

They see the differences between the morning, afternoon or evening business when you weren't there and all of a sudden there is this key member of the community standing in the middle of the casino floor looking like Colombo with that 'I'm watching you' look on their face.

Look, listen and learn when you get done eating lunch one day. Smile while you walk the casino floor and look at the key things I'm about to share with you. Never, I mean, never just go in front of the team members as if you are looking for things to write someone up or worse off make team members feel like they are going to get fired.

This is one of the morale busters that will only hurt your business in the short term, but even a short-term hurt in our industry means real money.

While look, listening and learning, here are some key places to go see for yourself (again, do it on your lunch break or during the next big event that your company or tribe is hosting at your casino):

1. Restrooms: You're only as strong as your housekeeping team. They are the ones that get to do the dirty work (literally) of making sure your entire property is clean. Sure you can look at slot machines or table games, where most of your money is being made, but if you have a great housekeeping team, they will keep your restrooms looking sharp and guess what, your whales and on the flip side those who are not gaming will have to do what.. eventually? Yup, use the restrooms! So, ensuring that your restrooms are debris-less, counters are clean and free from dead soldiers and especially urinals and toilets are immaculately clean is essential.

2. Slot and Table Games Chairs are pushed in: Look to see how well your casino team pushes in slot chairs and table games chairs. Surveys prove that gamers like to play slot machines that look like no one has sat there before or had the chance to hit the big one. Therefore, if the gamer thinks that no one has sat there because your team has done a good job of straightening out the chairs, (removing dead soldiers and emptying ash trays) then there's a good chance that the gamer will take a seat, pull out their wallets and begin making you money. Table games chairs

have a habit of inching closer and closer to the walkways where an even slightly intoxicated guest could trip and fall. Trip and falls are one of the most frequent small claim court issues that your company has to pay annually. Pushing in table games chairs not only saves you money in less frequent trips and falls, but esthetically it's more pleasing to the eye when you see things put in their proper places.

3. Lines: All casinos have some sort of line, whether it's at their rewards club, cash cage, restaurants or at a headline show in your event or banquet center. What you're watching for here is to see how long it takes a person to get through the line. Since you probably don't work at the casino, you may consider getting in line yourself and go through it. Look at your phone watch or better yet hit the start button on the phone's timer. You are really looking to see how long it takes and if the line gets you through in under 2 minutes, you have a stellar team working to make sure that your guests' wallets are not sitting in their pocket or purse and therefore you have a better chance to get more of the guest's wallet share.

4. Casino Signage: Make sure that all of the casino signage is updated. Look to see what the dates are on each piece of 'collateral' (which is lingo for poster, flyer, table tent, etc.). Marketing teams sometimes get lazy or don't have a system in place to update their collateral which makes the sign ineffective. Your casino could've had a new event that didn't get the love and exposure it deserved because your

marketing team forgot to change out the outdated collateral.

5. Just Listen: While you were in line, hopefully you paid attention to the words that were coming out of a guest's mouth. You don't have to wait for them to speak for you to gain more understanding of your casino product. Heck, if you want the information, then simply ask your guests what they think of the property. Act like you aren't from that tribe or have any real ownership (that way they will be more inclined to give you more information on what they really think of your product) and just simply say, do you like coming here? Or ask them what their favorite part of the casino is and why. Asking why is the most important part of 'the ask.'

6. Take good solid notes: While watching your casino floor, make sure that when you are done capture your thoughts on paper, a napkin or perhaps on your phone's notepad. Here's what you want to ensure you have when you leave the casino:

    a. Date/time/location: this is so important because let's say you did find some good nuggets of information where the product (guest service, atmosphere, food quality) was so poor that you really wanted to let your CEO know about it. Make sure you write down the date, the time and where you were at in the casino when you looked, listened and learned. If you have a great CEO, he/she will want to make this right but unless you wrote the team member's name down (hopefully they were wearing a name tag) how can the CEO do anything about coaching that team member? Far too often, I've heard tribal members or council members say that the casino's service 'sucked' (which is a real leadership term for "I don't know how else to be more specific but it made me mad to see this or that, lol) **but how can you expect leadership to do anything unless you tell them the specifics of the items that you are learning?**

b. Be as descriptive as you can by using good adjectives (words that describes the person, place or thing). Rather than saying the food quality was terrible, say that the texture of the clam chowder was thin or that the soda didn't have any carbonation and tastes bitter. The more descriptive you can write down, the better.

c. Write this down ASAP. There's been many times where I would go to another casino property and find all of these great things that I could bring back to the casino but failed to write most of them down. I would be asked how the casino shopping went but I would have incomplete notes. Make sure that you either keep a voice recorder handy, go to the restroom and speak into it or better yet, while you sit down somewhere (to have coffee or at the slot machine) text into your phone's notepad what you need to remember.

What you've learned here are just the basics of gaming, things that executives should look for daily in their areas of the casino. Here are some good questions to ask your CEO about the basics of their gaming day and what role they play:

1. Please describe your daily activities starting from where you park and how you come into the casino (here you are wondering if he/she takes any time to walk the casino floor to look for the things that you learned in this chapter).
2. What do you do when you personally see something that doesn't look right on the casino floor?
3. Do you casino shop other casinos in our market? Why or why not?
4. Describe our casino's housekeeping schedule? Do we have one? Here, we are looking to see how many times they clean the restrooms, which I've stated is the basis of how strong your housekeeping team is.
5. What aspects of our casino floor, granted you had all the money and resources necessary, would you like to change about it and why?

Chapter IV: Changing of Business Culture

What is business culture? Most of us Native Americans know culture simply by going to our annual winter or summer gathering.

In business, there isn't much difference, with the one major common element being human beings. Business culture is the way people act when the bosses aren't around. Hopefully your business culture isn't 'while the cats away, the mice play'.

Hopefully it's more to the tune that when the Boss is away, the rest of the 'team' (please don't call them 'staff', they are *your* team) is working hard, meeting deadlines, working together to accomplish the business's mission statement.

Mission statement? What the hell is that? Ok, ok, I'll admit most businesses don't do this anymore, but some of us old school thinkers still believe in the Mission Statement-the statement that describes just that-our mission!

Business culture stems from leaders in the organization; mostly their attitudes, their work habits, their paradigms (the way they think and act) all trickle down into the cracks of each team.

Some people, when they go from one casino to the next can see the major shifts of business culture. You can see it more or less when the team members are interacting with the guests.

If the business culture is one where the guest service is spotty at best, you can be assured that the boss's attitude about details is spotty, at best.

Conversely, if the guest service is amazing, they are hitting all of their detailed 'income producing activities' or IPAs as I like to call it, then you can rest easy that you know the person at the helm also believes in details and execution.

Out of all of the action items that it takes to create a better business culture, I would say the most important one is evaluation. I know that most tribal governments do not do much of this, but in business knowing where you are at in terms of performance is crucial to the future success of your business.

How will you know where you are going unless you can take a snap shot of where you are at today?

Evaluation doesn't just show you how far you have left to travel to get to the next destination, but it gives your team crucial feedback in terms of their performance.

Do you know why most people leave their current jobs?

You'd think it was about money? Nope. The two most frequent reasons why people find jobs elsewhere are high anxiety and boredom.

Once I was in a job as an Executive at a casino when a new CEO was introduced. We hit it off at first, but as time went on; and I, being the outspoken person that I am, disagreed with a decision of his to cancel an event that was to take place a few days later, we drifted apart.

From that point on, I didn't feel that I had a voice and moreover, I felt he was going to remove me because as he put it, I wasn't *his* guy.

How did that make me feel? Every day from that point on, I felt that I had a bullseye on my chest (not my back, but my chest). When you have a bullseye on you, it can make anyone feel high anxiety.

Boredom is another reason why people leave their jobs. Why? As human beings, we're built to want to grow. We are born, then we learn to crawl (or in my case I learned to walk before I learned to crawl), then walk, then talk. We do all of this because we're human and we like to grow.

That need to grow doesn't stop when we're 15 and puberty hits and now we're done growing.

As professionals, boredom is an employment killer because when we stop growing, we decide that we've done all we could do here and it's time to move on. However, most don't decide to move on and simply become average team members for your company. Average team members mean average production (avg. guest service, avg. cleaning, avg. dealing, etc.).

One of the best decisions I made was to leave that job at that one casino because high anxiety and boredom set in.

The perfect remedy to high anxiety in your team members is COMMUNICATION. Look within your team mates and ask them how they are doing. If they give off any sign of anxiety, calm them down; ask them what you can do to relieve that. Perhaps, they are not feeling comfortable with the job they are doing and they are afraid that they will lose their jobs.

Calm them down. Re-assure them everything is going to be great as long as they continue to execute your plan.

Teaching your teammates new things is another way of relieving boredom. Challenging them to increasing their secret shopper score, or getting through their lines just a few seconds quicker is all the difference in keeping your best team members around and not letting them go to your competitor.

As owners of the casino, our jobs are to ensure that our leadership is providing the best business culture for our team members. We need to be assured that there is a process in place to evaluate, monitor, set the direction, monitor, tweak the process here and there, monitor, and repeat.

We need to know that our leaders: Our Chief Executive Officer, our Directors, our Managers, our Supervisors (whom I refer to as our field generals) are all doing their part to help our soldiers on the gaming floor and in our non-gaming amenities grow.

Building a strong business culture through our team members is essential to the growth of our business.

What happens when a business has a weak business culture?

Man, I really didn't want to go into this, but here we go.

No Peanut in the Center Culture Leads to Lost Revenue

What if your leadership at your casino fails to do what I'm talking about above? They don't evaluate where they are currently, they don't set the direction, tweak it here and there and monitor more…

What you have my friends is a peanut M & M without a peanut. The peanut is the whole reason why I buy the Peanut M & M's! The peanut is the protein that fills you up and makes you healthier.

Have you ever been to a casino and felt that you didn't get your money's worth? The guest service was lacking, you didn't feel like the casino was clean or safe. Yeah, I'm raising my hand too.

When the quality of your business is down, the guests see that; heck they feel it. They know exactly what value they are getting for their money, but more importantly, what they are getting for their time.

It is our jobs as owners of the business to watch out for an empty peanut M & M. This is where we hold our CEO in check for ensuring that every single M & M has a peanut.

What are some key questions to ask your CEO when it comes to your business culture?

You may have a CEO who is very good, I mean; extremely good, at presenting a positive face to what is happening in your casino. He or she may do their presentation, give you the good story and hope that you don't ask these essential questions:

1. What evaluation process do 'we' currently have in place to monitor our guest services?

2. What are your key performance indicators (KPI) that you use to monitor the trends that you are seeing?

3. How do you define 'business culture.'

4. Do you evaluate your team's satisfaction of working at our casino?

5. If so, what are those KPI's?

These are just five questions to ask out of probably 100 that your CEO needs to answer from time to time.

In summary, I hope you gained a little bit more insight on how to effectively look at your casino and how the business culture should run.

Chapter V: Total Quality Management

This chapter talks about total quality management, short for 'who the heck is going to ensure that whatever product we're putting out there for the general public is worth a darn.'

Total Quality Management..wait for it, here's another acronym (TQM)...is basically the way you test and judge whether or not the product, service or 'otherwise' represents your best performance.

I had a CEO who did TQM every single day, especially at lunch, by looking, listening, tasting and learning about the products and services we were offering. Most people, eh hem..some tribal people thought this was not buying from the company, but in reality, it was TQM.

If a person who is judging the service and product was just going into one of our restaurants and eating food they didn't pay for, then yes, this should be considered stealing.

However, TQM is taking a ganders at whatever it is that we're selling (for a profit, mind you) and making sure that it is to his/her standard of quality.

Guess what?

If it isn't up to par with the CEO's expectations, what happens? You best believe the Director of that team should be sitting in front of the CEO jotting down notes as to what the CEO is saying needs to take place.

TQM is so essential to the business because it keeps every person who touches that part of your casino *in the know*. TQM is one of the most essential feedback mechanisms that you can ever get and saves your property so much time and money because if the CEO is good, which my former CEO was amazing at total quality management, he/she will 'stop the bleeding' before it can hit the next post on Yelp, TripAdvisor.com or Facebook.

As we'll mention in the Marketing chapter of this book, referral marketing can boost or sink your business quickly. TripAdvisor and Facebook are all types of referral marketing tools.

Most of what people put on those social media sites is not good for the business, but in reality will the Director really listen to a housewife from Missouri who lost her butt on the Craps table or listen to your CEO?

Yes, it's a cost of doing business, your Chief Financial Officer may have a hissy fit over the comp cost, but in the long run, it will be in the best interest of your casino.

Failing to have TQM could be the loss of so much revenue, mainly because the person(s) who have the most to say about the direction of your company may not know that the quality of the product or service that you offer isn't up to par.

When the quality isn't good, nine times out of ten, your guests know about it, have told their friends and relatives about it and they begin to play or dine somewhere else.

Your CEO should be look listening and learning all about your products and services; whether or not he or she does it as much as my former CEO (daily) or once a week or once a month, there should be a system in place for him or her to do this.

When the CEO decides to do this, they need to ensure that they are tasting and touching as if they are a guest in the casino. When they remove the politics, the personalities and focus strictly as if they didn't know the persons that were helping them, then they have the full opportunity to feel the experience like your guests do.

Now, we know that the nervous server who was given the daunting task of waiting on the big boss may give his or her most stellar service and the head chef or line cooks all know that the CEO is at table 10; but disregard all of that. Why?

This is due to the fact that even if the hamburger that the CEO ordered was created with team members knowing the CEO was in the house, that hamburger better be one of the best burgers ever cooked.

If it tasted just ok, then it's up to the CEO to tell the server who then should relay back to the chef that there needs to be improvements.

A good CEO would also take notes and ensure that he or she speak directly to the Food and Beverage Director or better yet, the F/B Director should be having lunch with the CEO so that this feedback may be given more quickly.

Total Quality Management is vital for the business to sustain itself and it's even more important that the CEO have the quality measurements to go by. If the CEO has never had great service or exquisite food, then how can they judge or measure their own team's service or food?

Not only should a good CEO be looking for the improvements, but also praising the good. For example, if the server did an outstanding job in service, then the CEO should publicly thank that team member for serving such a great meal.

If the food did taste really good, then perhaps a handwritten note to the chef letting her know that the food was amazing is in order.

Our team members are always looking for ways to improve, but more importantly, they need that positive reinforcement as well to let them know that the work they do is important and that they nailed it.

How do we expect our team members to know that they did well if we don't tell them? The note from the CEO will only carry more water when it comes to this and the servers, the chef, the host, all of them will know that they did a job well-done and replicate that when the bosses aren't there.

Here are some questions to ask your CEO the next time you meet regarding Total Quality Management:

1. What does Total Quality Management mean to you?
2. When you go into one of our restaurants to eat, what do you look for?
3. How do you give feedback (positive or improvements) to our F/B team?
4. How many times a week do you check for quality in all of our areas of our property?
5. What TQM measurements do you look for in other properties in our market?

Chapter VI: What is Profit?

You own a casino; in-fact you own a very lucrative business that generates millions of dollars annually. Do you know where your money goes or at least you should. This book isn't about what to do with the profits you are getting from your casino, that's up to each of the tribal council members that are elected.

Let's start with what is profit, after all that is why we get into business is to generate money that actually comes back to us, right?

Revenues-Expenses=Profit.

What are revenues? Revenue is the money that comes into your casino, all money. Revenue generators are the income producing activities (IPA) or activities that produce income for your casino. Revenue generators are not just the money at the slots and table games, but <u>all</u> the money that comes in. Every penny that is generated at any POS or point of sale system is the revenue that comes into your casino.

One revenue generator that some CEOs forget is banquet space. You can make a lot of money using this as true revenue generator.

That means every spa treatment, every hamburger, every beer, every ticket that is sold and a consumer is buying it, is revenue into your casino.

What are expenses? The number one expense drainer that you have to account for is what? No, it isn't that trip for 2 or that Mercedes Benz that your Marketing Department is giving away. Payroll is your number one expense. Why? Because the old adage, it takes money to make money rings so true in our industry.

You have to pay people to offer that service to your guest. You have to pay good people, good money to keep them at your casino. Your competitors are shopping you, or look, listening and learning to what your casino operators are doing or not doing.

Not only are they watching you, they are watching your superstars. They are hoping to attract superstars like the ones you are currently paying for. Most casinos operate with hundreds of team members; each one probably makes an annual salary of at least $35,000 per year.

As an owner, it behooves you to know and understand your revenues-and your expenses because these are some things that your CEO can control.

The Uncontrolled Revenue and Costs

There are some aspects of revenue that you cannot control, believe it or not. If you are in an area where you depend on another country's dollar value then you really cannot control that value. My tribe is located in the upper section of Washington State, where the Canadian dollar affects a ton of the revenues coming in.

For a long time, we took the position that we didn't want to depend on the Canadian dollar because guess what, the value of their dollar isn't controlled by us. Why depend on something that cannot be controlled?

Unfortunately, my tribe decided that they wanted to go after the Canadians because there were millions of potential guests that *could* come down and spend their money with us. Just like we forecasted, the US/Canadian dollar declined and over a million British Columbia residents decided not to even make a trek into the US since the value of their dollar was worth less. And, like I had told them not to do, they still threw good money after bad.

We cannot control the value of the dollar, darn, I wish we could go to the Bank of Canada and force them to set the rate of the US/Canadian dollar to 100%.

Another big uncontrollable item is the US economy. Kudos to you and your tribe for offering to take the risk on a big time business such as gaming. You are providing jobs where the economic impact is four times, five times and sometimes up to seven times what you are making yourself.

The people that you hire spend money out in the greater communities and pay for other jobs and so forth. So, congratulations for helping to enhance the US economy.

I wish it was that easy where we build the business and bam, our US economy is strong and revenues are to be had for all who are participating.

Change in US Government has a big part in determining the US economy; a new President sometimes makes those who invest in the economy shaky or perhaps the new Congress enacts laws that make it harder for small businesses to succeed.

The key performance indicators that we need to keep our eye on are the unemployment rates and discretionary income. When the unemployment rates of the people around your casino goes down, guess what, they do not have money to spend on entertainment.

The last time I checked, gaming falls under that entertainment category.

The good news is that when the US economy falters, gaming and drinking are usually the last two things that consumers will pull back from. It is my guess that when the crap hits the fan, the consumer wants to forget about his or her financial problems with a Bud…the beer and the slot machine, two buddies.

The Controllable Costs

I am thankful that when I was hired on at one of the casinos I worked, I had come in at one of the most inopportune time of my career. It was November, 2007, when I had my first day. By January 2008, the world's economy bubble busted and boy was it turbulent times.

We had weekly meetings to discuss what costs we could control to get us through those tough financial times. We had only given the tribe its minimal 'legal' disbursement of funds which was like $25,000 of profit. They had budgeted probably 10x that amount at the time, and so it was a very tense time for all of us.

One of my mentors told us in our first meeting regarding the controllable costs that he remembers back in the 1980s, his boss told them that they had to watch every penny. He said they would have to go to him if they wanted more pens to use in their offices to help run their casino.

Wow, I couldn't imagine having to ask for such small, mundane items like a pen.

It was the right thing to do, however, to make sure that all pennies were accounted for. They say every penny that you save is a penny earned. During those rough economic times, that truth couldn't be clearer.

As an owner of a casino, knowing how to save your money or at minimum questioning every line item is important. Knowing that your payroll is your number one expense, ask good questions about how much each department director is making and if it's in line with the industry average.

If a particular number looks off to you, do not be afraid to ask your CEO why that number seems high or what is the factor that makes that number so big.

You pay your CEO to ensure that the budget is in line with the forecast that you all agreed to at the beginning of the year.

One question I get a lot is this: during a time of consecutive quarters where revenue is down (which is called a recession, by the way) do you remove part of the marketing budget?

The answer I give is: HELL NO! The last thing you want to do is to remove one of your revenue drivers. Marketing consists of: advertising that big promotion; creating fun and interactive promotions to win a series of medium to big sized prizes to a high quantity of people and creating special events to bring people into your casino. All of these items cost a lot of money, but that is why you hire the best Marketing Director or Vice President of Marketing who can recommend the best ways to spend those dollars.

Summary

Remember revenue comes into your casino in various ways. Expenses go out of your casino. Both revenue and expenses can be controlled though some cannot be controlled.

Here are some important questions to ask your CEO when it comes to profit:

1. Why are profits up or down?

2. What are the casino's main revenue generators and what aspect of our casino is generating the most profit, other than slots and table games?

3. What are the main expense drainers?

4. Explain the current process for making a decision to make more revenue and conversely the current process for making decisions on spending our money.

5. Ask yourself: Does it cost money to make money? If it does, then how do you minimize the costs so that you can make more profit?

Chapter VII: Marketing: Promotions, Reinvestment %, New players, New Whales

When profits are down (more specifically revenue is down), the first place that most tribes look at is their casino's marketing department.

'Something's got to be going on with that Marketing team...!' exclaims the more vocal council member.

'Maybe we're not giving away enough cars, or enough coupons!'

Before you pound your fist on the table in despair, consider a few things before going down the road of spending the farm to get a skinny cow:

1. Look at your year over year trend analysis. Is it down by over 10%? For how long has it been down? One week? One month? One Quarter? Remember, a recession is three consecutive months of reduced revenue.

2. What's going on within 20 miles of your property? Was there a new business (including movie theatres, or any type of entertainment) that opened? Has unemployment went up in the past few months? Your business is competing with other entertainment industries and you need the people who live closest to you to have discretionary income to play at your casino. These are called key economic impacts that can affect your business rather quickly.

3. What's going on in the stock market or currency exchanges? These uncontrollable issues can drastically reduce your casino's revenue as your oldest guests (which

are probably your bread and butter market) depend on stocks to give them short-term dividends (money) and if your business depends on currency (Canadian or Mexican), you need to watch how the currency exchange affects your revenue-in.

4.　　Other casinos: Check to see what the other casinos are doing around you. Perhaps their re-investment percentage (we'll go through this) went drastically high. Perhaps, they were at a reasonable 15%, now they went up to 20-25%.

Having your finger on the pulse of the issues we've just raised, will help you consider your next moves.

With all things being equal, now you have to consider doing something to increase your marketing initiatives, for if anything, to match your competitors.

One of the golden rules of marketing that you need to consider when thinking about what to do to enhance marketing is this:

"What you giveth, you cannot taketh away"

I've seen it countless times where a casino gives away a ton of coupons (which I call 'papering the market') or giving automatic discounts by simply coming to the casino and using your player's club card.

What your casino gives, you cannot take away without having some sort of temporary or even permanent backlash by your guests.

'Well, I got that discount last Monday, why can't I get it today?'

'My husband gets that coupon, why can't I? I know I play more than he does!!'

Marketing teams have to recognize that when dealing with coupons or discounts, you have to consider the long-term effect of spending that money.

Sure, coupons and car giveaways are a cost of doing business, I am not recommending that you don't do these strategies, but just know that whatever you do, it could be perceived by the guest that you will always give them that coupon or discount; or be eligible for a new car.

Purple Cow Your Casino

Okay, just because I am from a tribe near many farms doesn't mean you have to get all personal with me. Lol.

One of the best marketing books available today is called <u>The Purple Cow</u> by Seth Godin. The premise of the book is to imagine yourself driving down a country road. Out in the pasture, you see grazing a pack of cow in the horizon. As you get closer, you notice that one of the cows in the herd is bright purple. You would remember where you were, who you were with, what was on the radio, where you going..etc.

The goal of purple cowing your casino is to do whatever you can to make your casino stand out from the pack. Think about it, all casinos have pretty much the same things: same slots, same table games, same types of restaurants, same spa services, same hotel services, etc.

This rule really has a lot to do with branding your casino in a way that stands out from the rest.

Branding is a very big aspect to your marketing efforts because of the long-term effects on revenue that it produces.

When you think of McDonald's, what do you think? You probably think, really good food, that is given to you really fast and is reasonably priced.

These thoughts and feelings about McDonald's is what drives people to come to their business and so they do everything that they can to protect and enhance those thoughts and feelings of its guests.

You too, have the opportunity to ensure that your CEO and Marketing team is doing whatever it can to protect and enhance your casino's brand through purple cow'ing it.

Look at every aspect of your current marketing efforts: snail mail, email, social media, TV and radio ads (these are all external marketing efforts) but moreover, look at internal marketing efforts. What are you doing on your casino floor that makes you a purple cow? Are you providing true world-class guest services consistently? Do you have fun and interactive (albeit quick) casino promotions?

Having the courage to stand out from the pack is very hard and almost got me fired from one of my casino jobs but I think it was mainly due to the fact we didn't communicate with the Council and business arm of the tribe before we hit the 'go' button.

Spend Money (but be reasonable)

Every CEO that has ever had the daunting task of driving headcounts up into the casino most likely started with their current re-investment percentage and then advised that they spend more to get more headcounts.

Re-investment percentage is looking at your current spend per player vs. how much the casino is getting back in terms of gaming revenue (mostly).

For example, let's say John Smith is someone who plays $100 in casino gaming (he's a part-time table games player but mostly plays slots). His average daily theoretical (ADT) or 'casino worth' is $100.

Note: Some casinos use ADT, others use 'Coin-In', or what is known as Slot Handle or Table Games Drop as a means to evaluate a player's worth to the casino.

If you were to give Mr. Smith coupons valued at $15, then you would have a single reinvestment percentage of 15%. We divide $15 into $100 and get the re-investment percentage of 15%.

Remember, however, that there was probably some other value-driven items that your casino gave him over the past three months. Mr. Smith was given a complimentary of $20 towards a restaurant, 2 tickets to your latest headline entertainment (valued at $50 total) and he got a $20 discount at the hotel.

Add all of this up and his cumulative re-investment would be what?

$15+$20+$50+$20=$105

Mr. Smith visited your casino six times in three months.

Remember that his ADT was $100 so he is valued at $100 X 6=$600.

Therefore, his cumulative re-investment percentage would be: $105 divided by $600 or 17.5%.

A reasonable reinvestment percentage is anywhere between 12-15%, but 'reasonable' is subjective to the aggressive nature of the market that you're in. If you know that your competitors are in the 20 percentile, then perhaps you better rethink your own re-investment percentage.

Buyer Beware

Just because I am recommending that you spend money on your casino players doesn't mean I am endorsing a full-on, full-court press.

Your CEO may say to you, yes, we want to put more money into marketing and so we'll up our mailers, we'll up our promotions and we'll drive in headcounts.

This all sounds great; being an aggressive casino is fun (for the short term). You feel a sense of pride that you are doing all you can to get more revenue for your casino and more profit for your tribe.

But...buyer beware. How much is all of this really costing your casino to do?

Here's the costs that you need to ask your CEO for to ensure that you really are getting a bang for your buck:

1. Mailers:

Printing costs: this should realistically cost your casino no more than .75 each (full color, full bleed).

Postage costs: this should cost no more than .50 each (may cost more if you are dealing with another country.

Value of each coupon: how much in casino 'funny money' are you giving up?

Design cost: your ad agency or your in-house creative team costs to create the mailer.

2. Promotions:

   a. Total cost of all of the projected or actual prizes given away.

   b. Total cost of payroll time it took to giveaway the prizes.

3. Player's Club Points and Tiering (also known as segmenting)

   a. If your casino offers tiering as a means to get people signed up for a new membership, what gives them incentives to go from one amount of spend to a greater amount then you have yourself a tiering club.

   b. Look at each tier: Gold, Silver, Bronze and General. Add up the value that each tier gives out to the players to see how much money that would be if the player was to redeem 100% of the offers on a single visit. Yes, it's true that not all players will redeem 100% of the offers in each tier, but this gives us our overall 'cost' per player per tier.

   c. You can then get a minimum qualifying re-investment dollar that each player should be giving to the casino (based on your established re-investment percentage, which I already said a reasonable re-investment percentage is somewhere between 15-20%.

4. On-going Discounts

   a. Your casino probably gives away a free buffet or something similar for their birthday.

   b. Perhaps you are giving away 50% off to guests 50+ on Tuesdays.

   > These are two examples of on-going promotions that you need to evaluate to ensure that your re-investment percentages aren't over the top.

5. Comps (or complimentary)

   a. Finally, the last and probably most expensive cost that the marketing department or gaming departments spend per player. Look to see your total comps given out in the past three months. Look to see what the overall revenue-in dollar amount is and do the math.

All five of these areas sound like a great idea to increase when your revenues and headcounts are lower than normal. You high five your CEO when he/she brings these ideas to your table, but you also need to know what the overall re-investment percentage is to ensure that you are not overspending.

Remember the branding issues that also get raised when you begin to get aggressive in your marketing spend. Are you helping your casino's cash flow in the short term to spite your long-term brand?

Referral Marketing

We'll be getting into more in-depth information about marketing in subsequent books, but before I end this chapter, I wanted to ensure that you know where Marketing is going in the future.

If your casino is not in the digital age, creating and focusing on digital collateral (your website, your social media (Twitter is a real-time conversation and if you're not going to spend money on a person who will monitor this 24-hours a day, then I advise you not to have one), referral websites like TripAdvisor.com and Yelp) then you better knock some sense into your marketing team.

Referral marketing is now becoming one of the most important aspects of driving in new revenue. Why?

Do you remember the last time you went to a movie? You probably heard from a friend or relative that that movie was good. You probably viewed the advertisement trailer on TV or social media a hundred times but since you trust your friend or your relative, you decided to go see that movie.

Referral marketing is going to be the central focus for businesses very soon, if it isn't already. One day, casinos will be paying high influencing people money to tell others why their products and services are x or y because of the fact we trust them over what's called push marketing

Push marketing is something that businesses have done the past century. We pay 'Creative Directors' a bunch of good money to design an advertisement that is going to look good, hope to make those who watch it feel good and hope that they come in after seeing that ad.

Sure, these ads do work, but in the next part of our century, more and more people will begin to look away from ads that don't serve them. Our on-demand services we're going to be getting will push out this type of push marketing.

Instead, marketing efforts will have to find a way to pull people into their casinos rather than pushing messages out. This is why referral marketing is very important and the strategy behind that will be a subject in the next book.

Just take a look at your casino's TripAdvisor.com, Yelp, Google +, Facebook and Pinterest social media sites. Check to see if there is someone from the casino responding to the posts that are being put on those sites by your guests.

If no one is responding, you better have a talk with your CEO about that.

Here are some questions to ask your CEO regarding Marketing:

1. Describe who our target market is: age, gender, ADT and re-investment percentage.

2. What is our current marketing strategy to target new players?

3. What is our current digital marketing plan and does it include referral marketing?

4. What is our direct competitor's cumulative re-investment percentage? (they may not know this to the exact number, but they should be able to tell you what your competitors do in each of these areas).

5. How are we going to be a purple cow?

Chapter VIII: Yes, Data is for More Than Tribal Elections

Ever heard the quote: Data doesn't lie? Well, data isn't the 'end-all be-all' but if used properly can tell a very good story about where you are at and allow you to set goals for where you want to go.

As tribal governments, the only times we ever really kept track of data was either for the annual tribal elections (how many voters there are and how many you needed to win) or for grants to help fund the services we provide to our tribal members.

Using data for businesses is still relatively new to Indian Country. Finally, more and more tribes are utilizing data to help them make better informed decisions.

The data that we will be talking about will specifically help your tribal casino in terms of these aspects:

1. Trending
2. Outliers
3. AB Testing
4. Overall Guest Worth

Setting You Up to Succeed

If your casino doesn't utilize data today, that's okay. Your casino is not that far back from the rest of tribal casinos in the US. Just because you're not that far back, doesn't necessarily mean that you should set yourself up to succeed.

There are a few very good applications your casino can use today that will help your business succeed:

(in no particular order):

1. Bally B.I.: The Bally Business Intelligence system is very good. Although there's been a few casinos that have dropped this application from their arsenal, the ones that have kept it say there is some really good tools that have helped them succeed in making solid business decisions.
   Bally BI allows a team to be able to see: Coin-In (see appendix regarding the casino lingo), table games drop, headcounts, jackpot totals, and more. If your casino has the Bally (Sci-Games is their new name) software system currently being used for your player tracking system, then the next natural fit may be this application.

2. VizExplorer: This application's creator came from the Bally BI team and you can tell that a lot of what the Bally BI tool can do can also be done using VizExplorer. The difference that I can see between the two applications is that Viz may be used for more than just gaming, which is pretty cool. They have subset applications that may be used for payroll (a business's number one expense), Marketing, and more. The people at Viz are cool and I recommend setting up a time to listen to what they have to say. Note: And no, this company nor did Sci Games pay me to put their product in my book.

3. Tableau: Their product does a great job of integrating many of the dashboards that you can get from Bally BI and VizExplorer but also including 'data in the cloud' features that allow teams from all over the world to access up-to-date information.

There are more data driven applications that all do pretty much the same thing. I always say that the pecking order of what you should be buying should be this:

1. Software System Support: Without this, you are a sitting duck when you have bugs (because every system has bugs) and you need a support system of people that will bend over backwards to work with your casino's Information Technology (IT) team to ensure that the system gets back up and running ASAP!
2. Functionality: Of course you need a system that will conform to your business's needs. Is the system you are buying a one-trick pony or does it have too many bells and whistles? Believe me, you don't want to over inundate your team with too many things that would bog them down from making the quick decisions they need to make.
3. User-friendly: Ever try to use a system that may have a great support system, great training tools, great functionality but in the end, your team has no real idea of how to consistently use it? Your data system needs to be user friendly so that those you expect to drive the car can instantly do that and they can easily train others to use it as well.

Non-System Supported Applications

Don't you wish you could snap your fingers and any tool that you need will just appear? Unfortunately for us, there aren't enough systems currently created that will help us do everything we need. One of those things that we'll need human energy rather than computing energy is in the area of headcounts.

Headcounts, which are different than door counts (more on that in a minute) are truly effective for many reasons. When your casino's team counts the number of heads that are in each revenue generating sections of your casino, you can see:

    a. What areas of the casino are consistently hot
    b. What areas of the casino needs more love
    c. Where signage should and shouldn't be placed for maximum effectiveness
    d. If any new promotions or couponing has worked

There are no laser beams right now that can track people as they walk into a certain section, and even if they did exist, how would you really trust that what you're tallying is what is actually happening?

The way your team should go about documenting headcounts is really quite easy but the execution could be your fatal flaw:

    1. Break your casino up into zones. Each zone should consist mainly of revenue centers (slots, table games, POS stations) and if you want to keep track of any non-revenue generating areas, then so be it.

2. Have a team of people who every two hours uses a tally counter to count the number of heads that they see in their zone.
3. Record that number in an Excel spreadsheet and save it in a shared folder for the team members you think need to see it.

Headcounts are vital to a casino because sure you can get an overall number using a door counter (laser beams that go cross the entrances of your casino property) but how accurate are those? Theorhetically, you could have a child go in and out (who was just trying to annoy a parent or who was bored) and how accurate was that?

Using the Data

Now that you have the data, now is the time to use it.

Using the software system or other systems (either automated or manual), ensure that you have a group of people consistently looking and analyzing the data.

Ensure that there is a person on the Government side (owners of the casino) and of course one or more people on the casino side who will review the data daily or at least weekly.

Why I recommend a person from the Government looking at this data and helping to analyze it is due to the fact that there are many CEOs across Indian Country that hire their own data person to pretty much only show the tribal owners the positives of what the data is doing.

It's uber-important to showcase the entire story and to be truthful about what is really happening in every revenue-generating part of your casino.

Here is what your data teams need to be looking at:

1. Trending: Until you get your data gathered over a longer period of time, you can look at the data weekly. Eventually, you want to get data that is looking back for a longer period of time such as month over month and especially year over year.

    Trending allows us to be able to see if a certain number called Key Performance Indicator or (KPI) are trending up or down. Similar to the stock market or gas prices, you can see where your KPIs are going.

2. Outliers: Outliers are KPIs that stick out from the rest. With all things being equal (same amount of time that you're reviewing, same ways of getting the data) all of a sudden you see a KPI that doesn't look right to you. The outlier may be an exciting number or it may be one that you wish you or your team didn't see.

3. AB Testing: AB testing is fun because you can actually use the data to test if a new product or service that you are doing is actually working. Using the data, you can see when you first implemented a new product or service and see if the KPI went up or down.

4. Overall Guest Worth: Gaming revenue will most likely make up over 80% of your revenue but a guest's worth is not just compiled of this number. Knowing how much a guest gives you for non-gaming revenue is also very important for at least one reason: building loyalty. If you know that your guest not only plays slots and/or table games but also visits your spa once

a week and eats at your Café twice a week, then you can see how much that guest is actually worth.

This overall guest worth is also important for the non-gamer as well and building loyalty with them. A dollar is a dollar isn't it; who really cares if it comes in the form of gaming or non-gaming revenue?

KPIs to Consider

Every CEO and Chief Financial Officer (CFO) has their own data and key performance indicators (KPI) that they use. KPIs should tell you how your revenue is being generated. For example, a key performance indicator not to consider would be headcounts in the hotel lobby. Although it's great that people like to sit in the lobby sofa and read a book, keeping track of that number really doesn't make business sense because those folks are not pulling out their wallets and handing you money.

Conversely, key performance indicators like: headcounts at slots, card-in percentage, slot and table games utilization rates, hotel occupancy, restaurant sales, spa sales are all great KPIs to consider when looking at your casino's overall performance.

Questions to Ask Your CEO

Hopefully you have taken my suggestion to heart about having your own data person. That person should be paid well because they are the ones that will keep your CEO in check. Ask that data person on your tribe's team to come up with the questions to ask the CEO at the next meeting. If your tribe doesn't have the money to hire a good data analyst, then here are some questions to ask:

1. Why did he/she use the KPIs to evaluate the business?
2. What other KPIs should we be looking at other than the ones we currently are using?
3. How far back do you look to compare the data?
4. Does our data tracking software have any bugs and if so, what is the support system process to get the data tracking back up and running when the data goes down?
5. Does he/she consider the guests' overall worth to the casino at all and if so, how do we track that?

Chapter IX: Guests' Interest and Profit

In reading the book Good to Great, author Jim Collins explains that businesses who went from good (they were in good standing in terms of revenue and overall profit) to great did well in staying simple and focused.

Those who stayed in the 'good' category were more likely to be all over the place in terms of their energy; trying to be all things to all people.

Casinos, like most businesses cannot be all things to all people. They can do what they can to expand their horizons in terms of being more of a general property, but at some point they have to appeal to a certain demographic.

Of course, that demographic (at least for most casino properties) is to appeal to the more affluent. You would never want to stop at just the affluent guests, for the $20 player (especially in high volumes) are needed to.

However, taking Collin's approach to going from a 'Good' casino to a 'Great' casino will take us thinking about how we make our business decisions.

In reviewing what made one of the former casinos I worked at go was the idea that we would make every decision with the guest's interest in mind and to ensure that whatever we did we made a profit on it.

Let's start with the first one.

Yes, the guest is always right; we've heard some form of this saying for ions of time, but do casinos really execute the idea that their guests are always right? Do casinos take time to listen to their guests or do they steam roll right over them to make that next dollar?

Understanding this principle that to go from good to great will rely on the guests is essential for the business to thrive and be sustainable over time. Relying on their input and listening to them takes discipline, something that again, most casino properties do not do.

Sure, they may get the monthly summary of the guest input cards (which are normally made up of the guests who were so fed up, so far gone that they want you to feel their pain). Most of what people say in input cards are filled with more emotion than message.

To gain a clear insight on the guest's message, it's imperative that your casino really listen; comment cards are not going to get you there.

Casino properties that truly care about their guests will spend time and money in getting the most feedback that they can get from two sources:

1. Focus Groups: Focus groups provide a great way for casinos to call time out and gain valuable in-depth insight on what moves them to come to your casino. You can get any third party company (or perhaps your ad agency if you have one) to conduct the focus group. You must make sure that the guests know that whoever is leading the focus group is perceived to not be a direct link to your casino; the guests will clam up if they think that the group leader is your direct team member.

The persons conducting the focus group should come up with a set of no more than 20 questions that they can ask in a 60 minute per group session (no longer than 1.5 hours, more than that and you lose your guests' interest and focus).

Go over that focus group questionnaire to see if they were properly worded correctly.

Here, you are looking for quality, not quantity; what this means is that we're not trying to figure out how many of x or y they are getting but more like how your products or services are being delivered. We want to hear from them how they are perceiving the quality of your gaming floor, the quality of your food and beverage, the quality of your housekeeping and so on.

Each focus group should be no more than 14 people in each session. We don't want to have too many people in the 'classroom' where one or two people who may be 'A'-type personalities will rule the roost. Remember, we want to hear from as many people as we can because there may be a nugget or two of information that will generate some revenue, if we only listen.

To get them to come to your focus group, you may want to give incentives such as: $100 free play or a dinner for two in your fine dining restaurant, an overnight stay; but keep that value of their time right around the $100 mark.

After each session is over, ensure that your leader and/or notetaker diligently writes down all of the items that pertain to quality. If it gets in there and a quantity remark is said over and over again, then ensure that is documented too.

However, the questions are asked, ensure that it somehow touches on the following: Ours and our competitor's Strengths; Ours and our competitors' Weaknesses; Ours and our Competitor's Opportunities and finally Ours and our competitors' Threats. This is a typical SWOT Analysis, but from a qualitative approach.

Once all of the sessions are over, ask the third party group who conducted the focus groups to see what trends were being said over the course of the six or seven focus groups that you are doing. Ensure that this information is given back to you within seven days so that you can go over things that may have come up that had you known about it, you would have changed it immediately. Sometimes, having the focus group conductors meet with you the last day they meet with the guests is essential.

Bonus: Not only should we be listening to our guests, but conduct an additional six or seven focus groups with your team members too; all frontline team members only. This will allow us to gain more insight as to what they are seeing but more importantly what they are hearing from our guests. We may see a huge trend in both sets of groups that we didn't see before.

The team member focus groups should use the same type of SWOT Analysis and we should also take a few questions to ask them how their working environment is going too. Happy employees make for happy guests.

2.   Social Media Websites: Yelp, TripAdvisor.com, Facebook and Twitter are all great sources of information that you can gain insight from your guests. Remember, that the trend in marketing is centered around guest referrals rather than paid advertisements.

We can gain a lot of insight from guests who may be writing to tell other potential guests about your casino property. There may be some trends that we notice that most of the people are writing about. Unlike the guest comment cards, most of what people say on websites like Yelp and TripAdvisor are done with the guest truly wanting to let others know about their experiences and are normally more balanced in terms of positive and improvements.

Once you have all of this great information now is the time to not ignore it. Collins also talks about having so much data to support a change in your business that you cannot ignore what the information is telling you.

Sticking your head in the sand because your business is not doing well, isn't a good example of going from good to great. Businesses must hear the brutal truth about what your guests are thinking about your products and you must have the courage to do something about it.

When we look at our food and beverage offerings, our process by which our guests are lining up for their entries at the player's club and all of these other things that we do in casinos, always make decision as if you were a guest.

The H-L-I Paradigm

When we make decisions with the guest in mind, we think of the three binding elements to making a profitable casino business, the H-L-I.

H stands for Housekeeping. Many people get amazed when I tell them that casinos are only as strong as their housekeeping team. Some laugh and think I am joking but in the end, your guests will perceive you care simply by seeing how well you keep up your home.

The first place that a guest makes this connection is guess where? Yup, you may have guessed it, the restrooms. If your housekeeping team makes cleaning all areas of the casino spick and span, especially the most dirtiest and visibly uckiest (this is a hospitality word meaning gross and disgusting, lol) places, then you will win this one.

Ensure that there is no dirty carpets, ash trays are emptied, dead soldiers (empty cans, bottles and glassware) are put away, slot and table games chairs are pushed in; all of these things go together in winning the H.

L stands for Leadership: There is a succinct difference between leaders and managers. Leaders think globally, they think process, they think with the guest in mind. Managers are scattered, they are not where you need them to be and are always chasing the carrot rather than letting the carrot come to them.

Don't get me wrong, there is a huge need for our team members to be managers. Managers do chase the carrot, but they also keep our front line team members in line and ensure that they protect the business through standard operating procedures or what's called internal controls (ICs).

Leadership who make business decisions with the guest in mind will go from good to great every time. Leadership should be the ones who may have come from the gaming or hospitality background. At minimum, your leadership should have some type of business background.

Your guests will know that your leaders care simply by the way the team members who work for the leaders are trained. If your team members are always giving the vibe that they are taking care of every guest every time, there is no telling how much repeat visits you'll get.

The more repeat visits you get the more opportunity you gain from attracting wealth and profit.

I stands for Information Systems or Information Technology (depending on what property you are at will determine what you name it). Now-a-days, with the slot and hospitality enterprise resource planning systems that most tribal casinos are buying into and the fact that your guests are looking for strong Wi-Fi connections makes IS/IT your new buddy.

<u>You are only as wealthy as strong as your IS/IT team is</u>. If you have a team that is not on the same page and moreover you have not put in the money to strengthen your infrastructure, then you will only stay as a good casino.

Great casinos have strong IT teams, so much so that when a system goes down, it's downtime is very minimal.

Recently, I worked at a casino where the slot system went down for upwards of four hours. FOUR HOURS! Can you imagine being the guest that was sitting on her hands waiting for someone to save her $200 slot ticket that was trapped in the slot machine for FOUR HOURS??!

That casino received a ton of hate mail and one star service reports on YELP and TripAdvisor. Remember, we are only as strong as our IT team is in getting the slot and hospitality systems working fully functionally.

PROFIT

Remember in our chapter entitled 'What is Business', we talked about what profit is.

Profit=Revenue-Expenses.

When we focus with our guests in mind and we focus on ways to increase revenue and decrease expenses, then not only are we perceived as the place where casino enthusiasts go, but we also are increasing our profit margins, thus gaining repeat visits and increasing wealth.

Balancing profit increases without hurting guest perception is very challenging. For example, let's say your guests want you to give away 100 smaller perceived items (say $50 per drawing, 100 times) but it would be cheaper to giveaway one trip for 2 to Hawaii (valued at $2,500), and you know that your market likes (not loves) trip giveaways what do you do?

Sure, your expenses are half the cost of the $5,000 daily drawing but if your guests are saying overwhelmingly to give away more smaller items more times, what do you do?

When you focus just on profit and not on the guests, you need to make sure that both of those circles integrate somewhere in the middle and make your decision that way.

For example, instead of giving away one trip for two for $2,500 expense, perhaps you giveaway an experience closer to home that costs you about $1,000 each and give away four of them. You saved $1,000 in expenses and you may have garnered just as much trip visits and profit per player.

Increasing profit wherever you can is good, but ensure that it's with the guest's best interest in mind.

Thinking about changing up your casino floor plan? Think with the guest in mind and profit.

Thinking about revising your menu in your fine dining establishment? Think with the guest in mind and profit.

Thinking about changing your ad campaign? Think with the guest in mind and profit.

Focus like a laser on these two simple but fundamental ways to go from good to great and you will increase your revenue and profit.

Chapter X: Per Capita

Ahhh...the million dollar question: To have Per Capita or Not? Since IGRA came into being, tribes have been dealing with this question, but really the real question is not about per capita, but success and wealth.

How do we deal with our success through the financial wealth that we have created?

We've been taught this poverty mentality where money doesn't grow on trees and that financial growth is stunted or limited.

So when the Creator sends us great people to help us create great products through the casino services and we start generating millions of new dollars, we as tribes have a really hard time knowing what to do with that new found wealth.

Tribal members all across the United States still endure through: highest unemployment rates, high diabetes cases, most per capita amount of people in jail or prison, highest suicide rates and so forth.

There really is a need to add resources to our tribal people to help them grow and to turn around these staggering statistics.

Teach a Tribal Member to Fish or Give the Fish Away?

The age old adage to teach a person to fish rather than hand the fish out is something that as tribes we need to figure out.

From a pure business standpoint, the stake holders or the general council (the voting members of your tribe) will continue to peck away at your casino profits year after year unless you get a handle on what you are doing with the profits of your casino.

I come from the standpoint that we live in a limitless world, that we can attract all the money and resources that we need or desire.

So, I'm not so hung up at the pure business standpoint more than I am more concerned with what type of people are we building when we give the fish away rather than teaching them how to fish.

We have generations of tribal members all throughout history that can remember the 'good old days' when they didn't have a pot nor a house to throw the pot out of, but they were happy.

Why were they happy?

I would argue that they were the happiest because life was simpler, they had a structure and they knew the order in which life is supposed to unfold.

You're born. You learn the cultural teachings. You make your elders proud. You contribute to the community through hunting, fishing and gathering; or being a speaker, singer or dancer. When you're too old to contribute, you pass on what you know to your youngers in your community and then you die.

Birth DASH Death.

It's that DASH that is the meaning of our lives. At our funerals, it will be the people closest to you that will define what that is through their stories; their laughter, their tears; all of this will come out at your funeral.

How did the casino profits contribute to that DASH? Did we just hand them a fish and hope that they take that fish to make jewelry out of the skin, can or jar the meat and sell it on Amazon and make millions of dollars? Or did they just eat the fish and look up for more fish from us?

As casino owners, this question of whether or not a tribe should be giving out per capita is probably one of the toughest questions that those who contribute these funds each year have to deal with.

I have yet to see a very successful per capita structure. I am sure that there is one that exists, but until I see that per capita contributions are going towards making a community more successful through these resources, I have to say I hope that more and more tribes decide not to give this out.

I have heard my community at Lummi Nation say that we shouldn't provide per capita checks because we are afraid of what they will do with that money. Maybe they will buy drugs or continue other hurtful addictions and one day kill themselves?

I have seen that per capita has been so big that the checks that the tribal member is receiving kills their initiative to want to progress such as getting a career or going to school.

I believe that this type of thinking is limiting (it may be true) but at the end of the day, a person will find any way to kill themselves slowly through their actions to make that a reality. Of course giving them money may make that process go quicker, but dying is dying; whether or not they do it quickly or slowly, the end result is still the same.

So, let's take that example: We shouldn't give per capita because we are afraid they will use it to kill themselves or others.

Even in the worst case scenarios where this may be true, doesn't it behoove us as the more responsible group of people who should be looking out for our community to begin to change this thinking around?

What is the root of that problem? Is it money? Is it a painful hurt that happened to that person as a child? Have they not gotten over a painful death of a loved one?

Money isn't the root of evil; EVIL is the root of all evil.

Money is a resource, a tool that we can use to help provide for our community; we can provide teachings, buy supplies, invest in our education and our culture.

I applaud those tribes who are currently doing this; I mean, they may not be fully giving out 100% of profits for funding things that could benefit the entire tribe (they may still give a portion of that money out in per capita) but they are trying.

The only way that this turns around is for the general council, the voting members of each tribe to decide that per capita is a hand out. That they are not entitled to that money in the form of a monthly, quarterly or annual check for the sake of being a tribal member.

A Hand Out is Not a Hand Up

Just plainly handing out money to our people is not conducive to strengthening our people for one main reason. I mean, we can bring up all kinds of reasons why handing out money isn't good but if we boil it down to one reason, it is this:

Not working for the money that we get breeds a lack of passion for life.

Huh?

Lol. Take a look at any person that won the lottery. They didn't work to get that money (although maybe they worked to buy that lottery ticket, but overall when that money comes in each month, they didn't work for it) and when you start seeing money come in without any real social, political, physical or mental equity put into it, it breeds ENTITLEMENT.

Entitlement comes from a place of lack rather than a place of abundance. Entitlement breeds more poverty mentality because poverty mentality says, I better get as much as I can, when I can because there if I don't speak up now to continue to get this money or even worse MORE money, then I will end up slowly dying.

A poverty mentality breeds a lack of passion for life. Think about it, when the money starts to roll in each month, whether it's $1,000 a month or $30,000 a month, would you want to work? Why would you want to do that?

Hopefully, if you come from a place of abundance, it shows you that this money that is coming in each month is amazing and you feel gratitude for the known and unknown sources it comes from, but it also allows us to do something amazing with it like give it away to a local charity, or start up a new health and wellness program with it.

When a person loses their passion for life, they start doing things with their lives that perhaps their elders are not proud of; perhaps it breeds a 'who cares' mentality. Who cares that I am doing this or that with this money? Who cares what my elders think about me?

A lack of passion for life breeds boredom. It's no wonder that many tribal members who do get this amazing money given to them start to do unhealthy things with their lives. They have nothing else to do; they don't go to work, they don't have a circle of friends to hang out with that contribute healthy things with their lives because they are too afraid that these 'friends' will take from them rather than give.

They wake up mid-morning, or close to noon, they went to bed late the night before, they don't eat healthy, they don't exercise.

Per capita when done the more traditional way breeds a lack of passion for life.

What If?

That's what I love about this book because I can explore the 'what ifs' of our industry and be able to give you value for the small amount of money it took to get your hands on this information.

What IF?...the profits gained from the hard work and dedication of your casino team members (tribal and non-tribal) went to fund tribal member's financial portfolio? The $500 a month that they are allotted, $50 a month went to a local financial firm dedicated to meet with your tribal member and set up their 401K, their tax structure and open their eyes up to investment opportunities.

What IF?...the profits gained from the monitoring of your casino budget from the council and senior executives went to fund small business opportunities for your tribal members? That money could go towards hiring a few amazing small business educators who can walk any and all tribal members through a 18-week program (held at your casino) designed to get them from their couch to owning their own business?

What IF? ...the profits gained from the millions of people who frequent your casino property went towards Life Advocates (AKA counselors) and Life Coaches? The Life Advocates (because you can't say counseling, or else your tribal member will drop the mic on that idea and leave) are funded to help our tribal members manage the oppression, the generational grief that has occurred and passed down from their elders.

The Life Coaches (AKA Guidance Planners) will be funded to help each tribal member who wants a better life, identify what that life feels like, help them remove the physical, mental and other barriers and be their biggest cheerleaders and butt kickers to ensure that they design their life rather than live their life with de-fault.

Most tribal members were taught to live their life in de-fault: which means they don't design their life but go throughout their lives floating and end results are just 'what happened by default' not be design.

Per capita, when done with the best intentions and with the best efficiency, can uplift not only this generation of tribal members, but sustain itself through the lifetime of our tribal nations.

Imagine what the hard working dedicated casino tribal and non-tribal team members find out that their efforts translated in the tribe teaching the tribal members how to fish rather than just a simple fish to eat for the month.

The success stories will continue to mount, the overall happiness of our People will start to tip in the positive way all because you helped provide them with teaching them about life, closing the message of their past stories, and overcoming the obstacles that are between their ears.

The goal is to answer that million dollar question of providing per capita or not with a resounding YES but in a more responsible and sustainable way.

Chapter XI: How to Manage Stress in a Business Setting

So you own a casino and you go to a quarterly update meeting and guess what? Your CEO says that you are trending down in various areas of the casino.

The CEO says that there's hope in a few areas, but overall profits are down year over year and they just got news that the local economy is projected to decline as well.

A local oil refinery which employs over 500 jobs is closing at the end of the year and they provided quite a boost in your gaming activity. They even supported your casino through various meetings held in your banquet rooms.

As a tribal council, you had already projected that the casino would provide your government with 40% more in revenue and now what?

The stress kicks in…you start to see your chances of re-election go down the tubes. Feeling a little light headed are we?

All of this feeling that you have within you is normal. BREEEAAAATHE INNNN>>>>BREEEEAAATHE OUUUT….ooooosaw! Rub your earlobes, it's going to be just fine.

Welcome to the world of business. Business, as much as you wish you could control the number of people who know about your casino, or control how much they spend once they come in is very cyclic.

Just like the beeper was once the fad of every 20-something, it's outdated now but here comes the smart phone. Technology, fashion, even the tides in the water tell us that what goes out must come back in.

You have to be ready for the day when your business is destined to sneak out of the norm for a while. If it didn't, it would defy one of the major laws that makes this world go around; the law of averages.

The law of averages says that what goes up, must come down. You see the law of averages in almost everything you buy, from gasoline, which a year ago was probably way up in price to the flight you just bought to Vegas. This is one immutable laws that will always be a part of the world we live in.

Taking Control of You

So, if you can't control the economy, the law of averages or at this point, it feels like you can't control anything, what do you do?

The only thing we can control is ME! Yup, that's right. You can only control how you feel about the news and the updates around you. Are you going to lose your shirt because profits are down? Are you going to freak out and say the sky is falling; should we nickname you Chicken Little?

No, you were born into a family that taught you otherwise.

Instead, you are going to control your emotions, not overreact and take three deep breaths.

Hopefully through reading this book, you've decided that you cannot depend on too many people to help you with your business. Although you depend on your CEO to take care and manage the people, the process and the product, you play a gigantic role in the ultimate success (or failure) of your casino.

How?

One way of controlling your stress is to educate yourself about your industry, your economy, new products, the price of important things like payroll (is it trending up or down in the industry?), slot machines, food costs.

Why wait and wonder what those things cost when you have every right, every ability to learn about this yourself?

Gone are the days when tribal council, tribal general council members (voting members of your tribe) sit back and wait for the information to come to them.

The real owners, the ones who really care, will do some damn research themselves through the little thing called the internet.

This is the best time to own a casino because now we have at our disposal, 24-hours a day the ability to read and research these questions on our own.

When you are ahead of your CEO or your community, you have the ability to take in any news or updates that make you freak out and be able to sort through the information in a more professional way.

Exercise and Eat Healthy

One of the best ways to take care of others is to take care of yourself. How many times a week do you take just 30 minutes and go for a walk or jog? How many days a week do you eat at least three times a day, especially breakfast?

You owe it to your family and most importantly to yourself to take care of yourself. I was so happy that I decided to do that and shed almost 25 pounds of excess fat that was around my belly (which is caused by stress). I had more energy, more thinking power and most importantly, I was able to take on a bunch of new stress that previously would've had me in the hospital.

As tribal members, we're already susceptible to diabetes (hate to say it but it's probably in your genes), so eating healthy and exercising is something we should already be doing.

For me, I eat more protein than I do carbs. I look for items in the grocery store that has a 'right-side up' protein to carbohydrates quotient.

Protein is awesome for you because it makes you feel full, it helps build muscle and gives you the needed energy throughout the day.

Finally, I eat protein in the form of beef jerkey, salmon, protein bars, peanut butter, tuna fish, anything that has a lot of protein at least once every three hours. I drink a ton of water and have the occasional cup of coffee.

Exercise and eating healthy are key to a successful life, but more importantly to a body and mind that will take on the pressures you're feeling about your cyclic business.

Meditation/Prayer

I believe that one of the best things that I ever did for me and reducing stress is meditation. I include prayer after I meditate, but boy, talk about a mind massage.

If you're anything like me, you probably have a voice in your head that is active and always chatting to you. Although it's easy for me to get to sleep at night (I can even sleep on a plane before it takes off), I needed something to shut out or tune out that voice so that I could focus on the next steps in my success.

Breathing techniques (deep breath in and deep breath out) are an amazing way to blow out steam, to reduce the stress that your active mind is dealing with.

When you breathe out these stressers, you feel your body and mind become so much lighter and you're able to fill your cup with more stress that day, rather than a feeling of excessive stress where you just want to scream at everyone in sight.

Prayer is amazing because you are calling on a higher power to help you and your tribe. You feel a connection with the Creator and know that this ultimate power is guiding you to help make your tribe better.

Stay Calm

One of the worst things you can do as an owner of a casino is to freak out. When you send the message to the CEO that the sky is falling either by yelling at him/her or threatening the CEO, guess what will happen?

Have you ever heard that the crap rolls downhill? It's an old expression that says that when you crap on the top of the hill (CEO), that crap will trickle down the hill (and onto all of the team members below the CEO).

Remove the crap, don't allow the CEO to be a tyrant because he/she is feeling the pressure of the tribal council to do better.

Stay calm, cool, relaxed and ask questions that are solid and will help the team get through this turbulent time.

Practice intelligence over emotions (I over E) where your smart side of you comes out and helps get your team on the right page, with the right actions to take.

Remember you were elected for a reason, because you get crap done and you do it with the proud ancestors watching over you.

Here are some questions to ask yourself regarding management of your stress in a business setting:

    1. What are your personal goals for health and fitness?

    2. What are your personal goals for eating healthier?

    3. How are you managing your time so that you can go from one meeting to the next without double booking or feeling stressed about being late?

    4. How are you managing your personal finances so that it is one less thing you need to deal with?

    5. Who do you talk to about the business updates and are they supportive of your decisions?

Chapter XII: Don't be THAT Casino...!

At the time of writing this book, one of the casinos that I was familiar with, announced that it had closed its doors.

As much as I pray for all tribal members whose casino closes, our goal as tribal members who own a casino is to NOT be that casino.

We need to ensure that our business is nice and healthy, that we are doing everything that you've read in this book, consistently, with discipline.

Discipline is a key word in the way that your business executes the plan that your tribe and your management team has. Without disciplined efforts, disciplined team members and disciplined thoughts, your casino could end up like this casino.

Here are some ways to ensure that your casino doesn't end up closing its doors:

- Casinos are a business and run them like one; they are not a government program. There are differences between these two types of things that we get to do on reservations.
- Hire GREAT people. When we hire great people (in terms of good heart, passionate about the industry, passionate about improving, communicative, etc.) to execute the vision and plan of the tribe and the management team.
- PAY great people. Yup, as much as your team members (including your tribal members who work there) may love your tribe and be thankful for having a job, you MUST pay them! I'm not talking about

gigantic contracts that are all guaranteed, but look at the industry average for each position and ensure that you are paying your team members at least the industry average. If the industry is saying that most casinos give bonuses, then give them. Let's put it this way, if you decide not to pay them or give bonuses, your competitors will and steal your great people from your casino.

- Have a championship mindset: As a tribe, we have the ability to help run our casino by having a championship mindset. We must believe in the teams that are assembled in our casino, have the faith that they will do the best of their collective ability, but leave them alone to do these jobs that we are paying them to do. One great tribal leader told me that his job as a council member is to let casino people do the work that they are paid to do. Paul Allen, the owner of the Seahawks doesn't get into the weeds and question the entirety of the team, he lets his coaches do their jobs and it's his championship mindset that allows the team to continue to win and compete for the Superbowl ring.

- Adjust, Adjust, Adjust: This is one of the most important aspects to not being the type of casino that closes its doors. You MUST collect the data, you MUST use the data, you MUST have brutal honesty about how things are going and you must ADJUST! Failure to adjust to market demands, to external uncontrollable forces (like the economy) is failure to be responsible and to have the discipline to make the necessary moves to thrive, not just survive.

Again, I appreciate the courage your tribe and you are taking in even having a casino. You get a pat on the back for reading this book and I encourage you to take what you've learned in the book and pass it on. Our casinos will not sustain itself over time if we don't have an abundance mentality that says lets educate each other on what we're learning. WE cannot horde the information and we cannot continue the poverty mentality that leads us to keep information, keep the profits for ourselves and not be good community members.

Cheers to your journey and to the continued success of your business and beyond!

Made in the USA
Columbia, SC
13 March 2023